Oxford International Resources

3

Skills

Writing and Grammar

Katie Southwell

OXFORD
UNIVERSITY PRESS

OXFORD
UNIVERSITY PRESS

Great Clarendon Street, Oxford, OX2 6DP, United Kingdom

Oxford University Press is a department of the University of Oxford. It furthers the University's objective of excellence in research, scholarship, and education by publishing worldwide. Oxford is a registered trade mark of Oxford University Press in the UK and in certain other countries.

British Library Cataloguing in Publication Data
Data available

9781382046084

10 9 8 7 6 5 4 3 2

Paper used in the production of this book is a natural, recyclable product made from wood grown in sustainable forests.

The manufacturing process conforms to the environmental regulations of the country of origin.

Printed in India by Manipal Techonlogies Limited

Acknowledgements

The publisher and authors would like to thank the following for permission to use photographs and other copyright material:

Cover: Andrea Manzati

Photos: p5: © Flaticon/Freepik Company; p6: DestinationsInNewZealand / Shutterstock; p8: HappyPictures / Shutterstock; p12: Vector Tradition / Shutterstock; p14 (r): SpicyTruffel / Shutterstock; p14 (l): Kucher Serhii/Shutterstock; p15 (tl): Yefym Turkin / Shuttesstock; p15 (tr): Yefym Turkin / Shuttesstock; p15 (bl): Yefym Turkin / Shuttesstock; p15 (br): Yefym Turkin / Shuttesstock; p16: GoodStudio/Shutterstock; p16: White Space Illustrations/Shutterstock; p17: GoodFocused / Shutterstock; p18: Sararoom Design / Shutterstock; p20, p43 (b): Zhanna Mendel / Shutterstock; p21 (tl): Steve Cox; p21 (tr): Constanza Basaluzzo; p21 (bl): Zhanna Mendel / Shutterstock; p21 (br): Zhanna Mendel / Shutterstock; p22: Natalia Sheinkin / Shutterstock; p24: Tartila/ Shutterstock; p26: ensiferum / Shutterstock; p28 (r): Eric Isselee/ Shutterstock; p28 (l): 0020_TI_10813-rf_DAM; p28 (m): Roger ARPS BPE1 CPAGB/Shutterstock; p29: Alexius Sutandio / Shutterstock; p31 (t): Anton_Ivanov / Shutterstock; p31 (b): imageBROKER / Alamy Stock Photo; p32 (l): Richard Peterson/Shutterstock; p32 (r): Eric Isselee / Shutterstock; p34: Valeriy Kachaev / Alamy Stock Vector; p36 (l): Shyamalamuralinath/Shutterstock; p36 (r): fotandy/Shutterstock; p37: Tupungato / Shutterstock; p38: Paper Trident/Shutterstock; p39: Zurijeta /Shutterstock; p40 (a): Volodymyr Goinyk / Shutterstock; p40 (c): Brent Parker Jones; p40 (b): Designs Stock / Shutterstock; p40 (d): Nattika / Shutterstock; p41 (a): Mark Ruffle; p41 (b): kyoshino/iStock/Getty Images; p41 (c): Dennis Kitchen Studio, Inc; p41 (d): Mark Ruffle; p41 (e): Anthony DiChello/Shutterstock; p41 (f): Constanza Basaluzzo; p41 (g): GARETH BODEN; p43 (t): Svetlana Rey / Shutterstock; p44: HappyPictures / Shutterstock; p44: HappyPictures / Shutterstock; p44: HappyPictures/Shutterstock; p45: PCH.Vector/Shutterstock; p46: Danilo Sanino / Shutterstock; p47: DVitaliy / Shutterstock; p53: Selena1981 / Shutterstock; p56: fizkes/Shutterstock; p59: Pixel-Shot/Shutterstock; p60: Monkey Business Images/Shutterstock; p61: mimagephotography / Shutterstock; p62 (l): Oxford Universtiy Press / Lindsay Edwards Photography; p62 (r): Monkey Business Images/Shutterstock; p64: Undrey / Shutterstock; p65: Anthony Rule; p68: Teo Tarras / Shutterstock; p68 (br): ju_see / Shutterstock; p69: FOTOKITA/Shutterstock; p70: Qualit Design / Shutterstock; p71: HitToon / Shutterstock; p72: Monkey Business Images / Shutterstock; p75: Cenz07/Shutterstock;

Artwork by QBS Learning, Robin Boyer, Anthony Rule, Constanza Basaluzzo, Mark Ruffle, Simon Clare, Michael Emmerson, Andrew Painter, Mona Meslier Menuau, Tim Archbold, Dan Gartman, John Abbot Nez, Micha Archer, Alexandra Colombo, Marcin Piwowarski, Jan Smith, Meilo So, Francois Ruyer, Hannah Cummings, Alex Brychta, Alex Steele-Morgan, Ayesha L. Rubio, Oxford University Press.

Every effort has been made to contact copyright holders of material reproduced in this book. Any omissions will be rectified in subsequent printings if notice is given to the publisher.

The manufacturer's authorised representative in the EU for product safety is Oxford University Press España S.A. of el Parque Empresarial San Fernando de Henares, Avenida de Castilla, 2 – 28830 Madrid (www.oup.es/en).

Contents

1 Ali is stuck in the desert. What dangers are there? What does he need to survive?

sand dune

palm tree

snake

bush

fish

water

2 Write some questions to ask Ali. Don't forget to use question marks!

Why are you in the desert?

3 Write the correct punctuation mark **(. ! ?)** at the end of each sentence.
Then match the sentence to the sentence type.

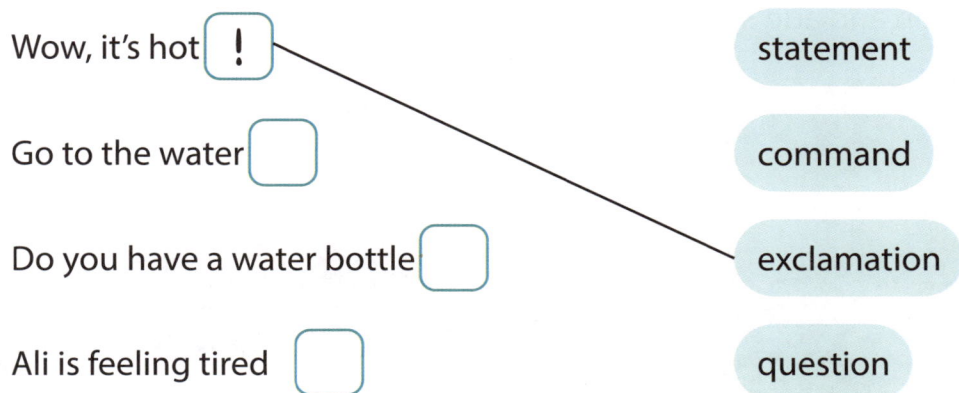

Wow, it's hot **!**   statement

Go to the water ☐   command

Do you have a water bottle ☐   exclamation

Ali is feeling tired ☐   question

4 Imagine that you can send Ali three things to help him survive in the desert. Give Ali
instructions for how to use them. Check that you have used the correct punctuation.

| material | rope | sun | hat | bottle | shade | tent | fishing rod |

Use the material and rope to make a shelter.

First,

1   Look at the picture for 1 minute.
    Cover it up, then discuss what you remember.
    Look at the picture again and add some labels.

2   Match each word to its word type.

calm   path

waves   lighthouse

sea   **Noun** | **Adjective**   tall

cold   rocks

bright   smooth

3 Fill in the gaps in these instructions for drawing the picture.
Use **nouns** and **adjectives**.

tall	sea	dangerous	~~long~~	clouds	sky	golden

Draw a _____long_____ , winding path.

a At the end of the path, draw a _____ lighthouse.

b Draw a _____ light, like a star, on top of the lighthouse.

c At the side of the path, draw some _____ rocks.

d Both the _____ and the _____ are calm.

e In the sky, draw some thin, pink _____ .

4 Imagine a different setting, like your bedroom, somewhere you like to play, or a place where you go for walks. Using nouns and adjectives, write instructions for how to draw it. Ask a partner to use your instructions to draw your setting on a piece of paper.

1 Use the pictures to discuss how to grow a plant. What do you do first? What do you do next?

Vocabulary

watering can   soil   spade   seed

_____ a hole.

_____ the seed in the soil.

_____ water over the seed.

_____ your plant grow.

2 Use these **verbs** to complete the labels.

Pour   Dig   Watch   Put

3 Choose verbs and **adverbs** to complete these instructions.

daily	next	~~dig~~	finally	watch	gently

1 First, dig up the soil.

2 _____, plant a seed.

3 Cover it with soil and pat it _____.

4 Water it _____.

5 _____, _____ your plant grow.

4 Write instructions for one of the following topics:

- brushing your teeth
- having a fun weekend
- leaving the classroom

Remember to use adverbs!

_____

_____

_____

_____

_____

_____

_____

_____

_____

1 Imagine that you could choose a dinosaur as a pet. Which dinosaur would you choose and why?

2 What might happen if dinosaurs came back to life? Complete these thought bubbles with your ideas. Use **pronouns**.

they   we   she   it   he   me   you

We might have to run and hide.

3 Match the pronoun to its **possessive pronoun**.

she	mine		you	theirs
he	hers		they	ours
me	his		we	yours
it	its			

4 Imagine that you decide to look after some dinosaurs in your home. Write instructions for your family using the pronouns: they, my, our, we.

food   bedroom   sleep   wash   space

We will need lots of space for the dinosaurs so I will give up **my** bedroom.

1 You're off to find treasure! Look at the map and talk about what problems or dangers you might face.

| desert | food | water | mountain | shelter | heat |

2 Use bullet points to write a list of everything you need to take.

• food

3 Using the headings, write some instructions for you and your partner.
Add your own heading for the last section.

| prepare | we must | we should | we will need | cold | food | water | lost |

Before we leave

We must tell someone where we are going.

_____

_____

Dangers we will face

_____

_____

_____

Heading: _____

_____

_____

_____

4 You have found the treasure! Use bullet points to write a list of things you will buy.

● _____

_____

_____

1 With a partner, decide which of you will be Captain Seadog and which will be Sailor Kareem.
What might you say? Act out a conversation.

Sailor Kareem, I have heard that a storm is coming.

Don't worry, Captain! We can sail through any storm!

Captain Seadog

Sailor Kareem

2 Rewrite the sentences below, replacing the word 'said' with a **synonym**.

| asked | moaned | ~~ordered~~ | shouted | whispered |

"Stay where you are!" said Zaynah.

"Stay where you are!" ordered Zaynah.

a "Try to stop me!" said Rafael.

_____

b "Shhh! We must be quiet," said Ameerah.

_____

c "I don't want to go," said Nadia.

_____

d "Where are we going?" said Imran.

_____

3 Add the synonyms to the correct box. Use the clues to help you.

queried   snarled   sobbed   cheered   bawled   laughed   barked

enquired   questioned   wept   bellowed   giggled

Questioning 🤔	**Sad** 🥹
q u e r i e d	w __ __ t
q __ __ __ __ __ __ __ __ d	s __ __ __ __ d
e __ __ __ __ __ __ d	b __ __ __ __ d
Happy 😃	**Angry** 😠
g __ __ __ __ __ d	s __ __ __ __ __ __ d
c __ __ __ __ __ d	b __ __ __ __ __ __ __ d
l __ __ __ __ __ d	b __ __ __ __ d

4 Imagine that Captain Seadog is telling Sailor Kareem off for not doing his jobs on the boat! Write their conversation using synonyms for 'said'.

wash   scrub   clean   deck   lazy   bed   cabin

_____

_____

_____

_____

_____

_____

2 Stories

1 Choose one 'Who, What and Where' from each column.
Tell a partner a story using the three things you chose.

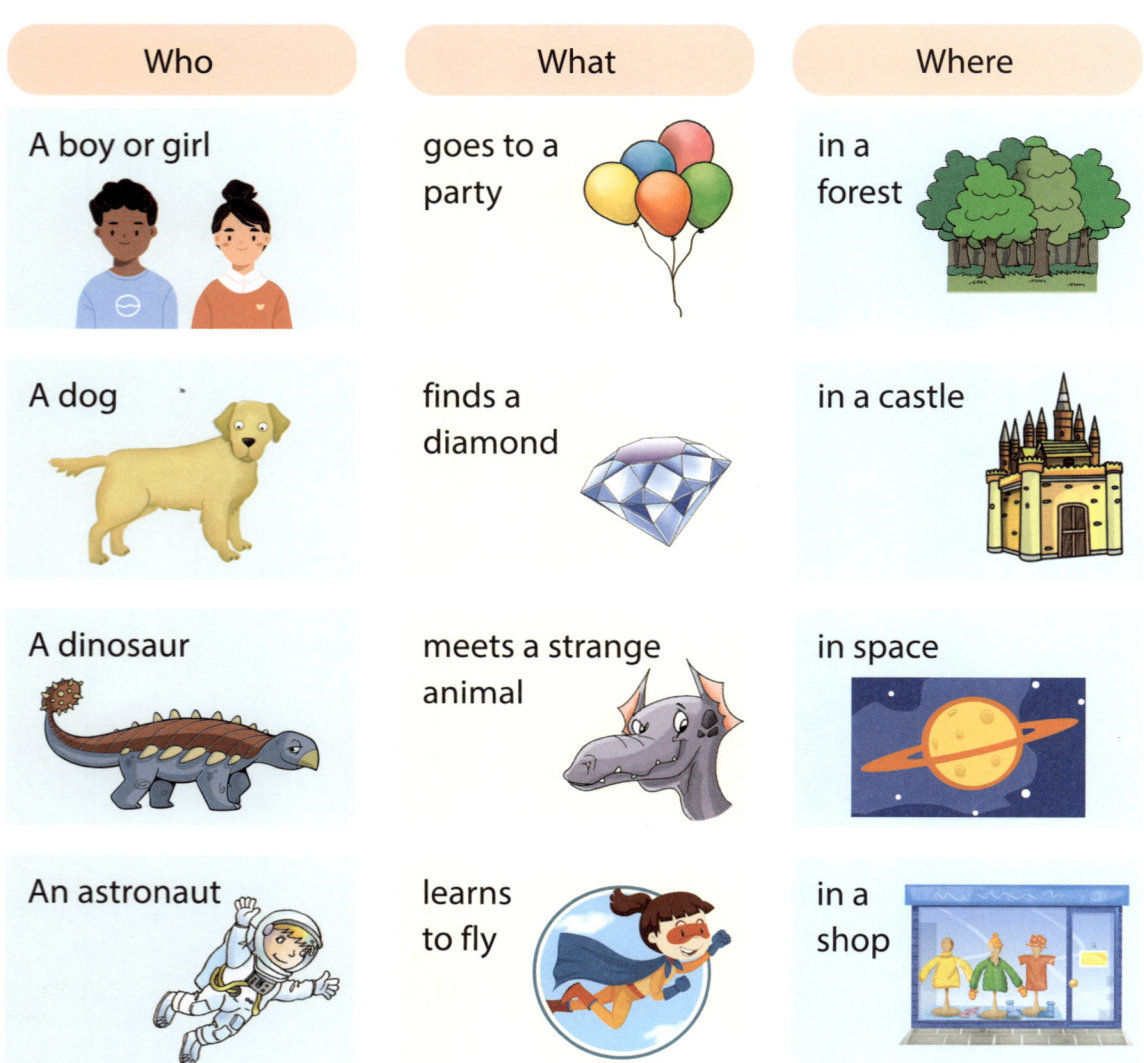

Who	What	Where
A boy or girl	goes to a party	in a forest
A dog	finds a diamond	in a castle
A dinosaur	meets a strange animal	in space
An astronaut	learns to fly	in a shop

2 Write your 'Who, What and Where' story ideas below.

A dog learns to fly in the forest.

3 Circle your favourite story idea from **2**.
Choose a name for your character: _____

What will happen to them?

Beginning: _____

_____

Middle: _____

_____

End: _____

_____

4 Write the first paragraph of your story. Include interesting details
about where your story takes place and your main character.

Once, there was a _____

_____

_____

_____

_____

_____

_____

_____

1 Look at the pictures. Retell the story *The Lion and the Mouse*.

2 Choose an **adverb of time** to fill each gap. Don't forget to add a comma after each one!

Then	Finally	~~Once~~	Later on	One day

Once, there was lion and a mouse.

_____ the lion was fast asleep in the hot sun.

_____ along came the mouse. Suddenly, the lion woke up

and grabbed it.

"Please let me go!" squeaked the mouse.

The lion took pity on the mouse and let it go.

_____ the lion became trapped in a hunter's net!

_____ the mouse helped the lion by biting through the net to free him.

3 Write these adverbs of time in order from earliest to latest.

> at midnight   in the middle of the afternoon   ~~in the morning~~
>
> after lunch   at bedtime

1 in the morning

2 _____

3 _____

4 _____

5 _____

4 What do you think happens after the mouse frees the lion? Write the next part of the story. Remember to use adverbs!

> friends   thank you   grateful   helped   favour   rescued

_____

_____

_____

_____

_____

_____

_____

1 Pick an animal. Describe it to a partner. Can your partner guess which animal you are describing?

2 Rewrite the sentences below, replacing the **adjectives** with **synonyms**.

| frightening | scorching | ~~tiny~~ | powerful | cheerful | huge |

Once, there lived a **small** koala.

Once, there lived a tiny koala.

a The crocodile had **scary** teeth.

_____

b The monkey swung with its **strong** arms.

_____

c The toucan had a **big** beak.

_____

d The lizard stood in the **hot** sun.

_____

e The **happy** hippo lay in the mud.

_____

3 Add the synonyms to the correct box. Use the clues to help you.

creepy   excited   horrifying   minute   fearsome   ~~massive~~

delighted   giant   mini   enormous   glad   teeny

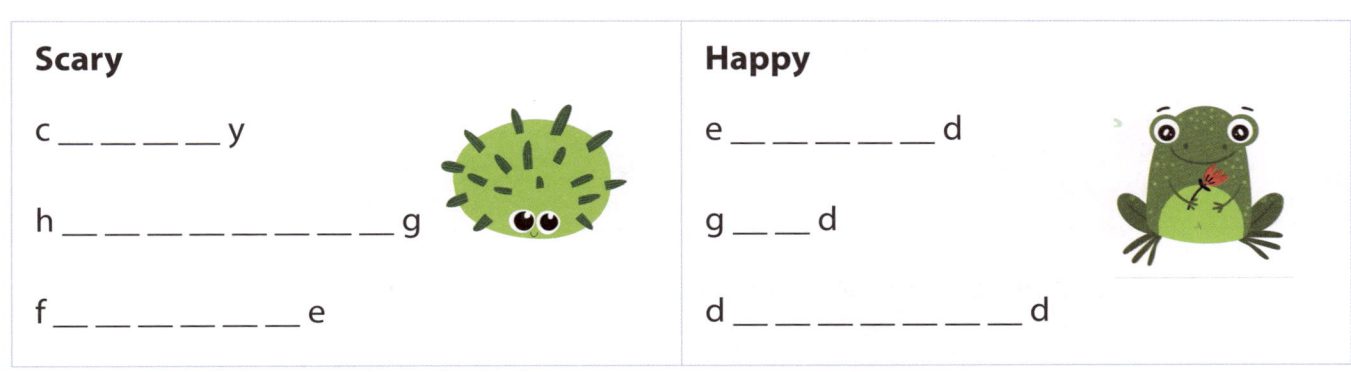

Big

m a s s i v e

e _ _ _ _ _ _ _ s

g _ _ _ t

Small

m _ _ i

t _ _ _ _ y

m _ _ _ _ _ e

Scary

c _ _ _ _ _ y

h _ _ _ _ _ _ _ _ _ g

f _ _ _ _ _ _ e

Happy

e _ _ _ _ _ _ _ d

g _ _ d

d _ _ _ _ _ _ _ _ d

4 Finish this story, using at least three words from **2** and **3**.

At the bottom of the tallest tree in the jungle, there

lived _____

_____

_____

_____

_____

1 Create your own funny pet! Discuss it, then draw it in the box.

5 mins

2 Add information about your new pet below. Use lots of **adjectives** to describe them.

Words to describe them:
-
-
-
-
-
-
-
-
-

Age:

Name of funny pet:

Dislikes:
-
-
-
-
-

Likes:
-
-
-

-
-
-

3 What is the bravest thing your pet has ever done?

_____

_____

_____

What is the naughtiest thing your pet has ever done?

_____

_____

_____

4 Write about your new pet. Include lots of adjectives to add interesting details. Your pet could meet your partner's... Would they be friends or enemies?

hairy   spiky   cheeky   stripy   grumpy   friendly   fluffy   kind   silly   sparkly

_____

_____

_____

_____

_____

_____

_____

1   Use your senses to describe this dragon. What does it look, feel, smell and sound like?

look

smell

feel

sound

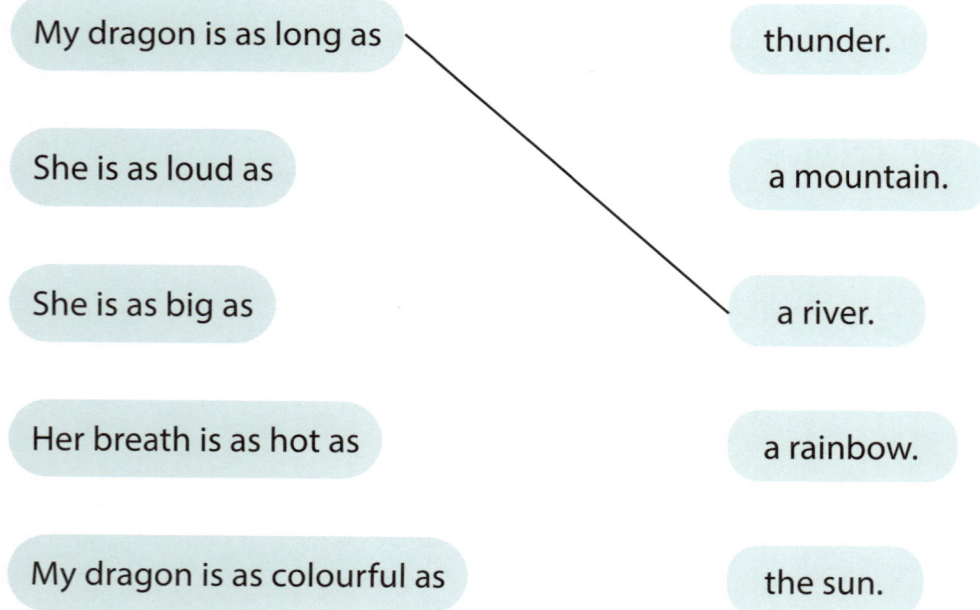

2   Match the beginning of the **simile** to the end.

My dragon is as long as

thunder.

She is as loud as

a mountain.

She is as big as

a river.

Her breath is as hot as

a rainbow.

My dragon is as colourful as

the sun.

3 Complete the first part of each simile using one of these **adjectives**.
Then add your own ending.

| sharp | twisty | ~~shiny~~ | strong | red |

a My dragon's eyes are _____shiny_____ like _____

b Her teeth are _____ like _____

c Her ears are _____ like _____

d My dragon is _____ like _____

e Her tail is _____ like _____

4 Write a story about a dragon. Use similes.

His fur is as soft as a cloud. _____

_____

_____

_____

_____

_____

_____

_____

_____

_____

_____

1 Talk about what it would feel like to be on a ship in a storm.
What would you see and hear?

see		hear

2 Make figurative descriptions by matching these phrases.

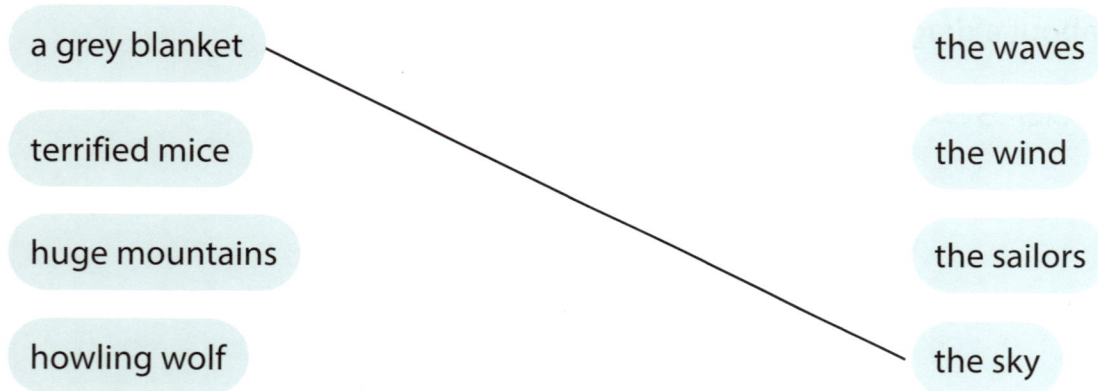

a grey blanket   the waves

terrified mice   the wind

huge mountains   the sailors

howling wolf   the sky

3 Write the descriptions above as **metaphors**. You can add **adjectives** if you like.

The sky was a dark, grey blanket.

4   Imagine you are the captain of the ship. Write your diary entry for the day
of the storm. Use metaphors.

Dear Diary,

This morning, we watched in terror as a frightening
storm rolled in.

_____

_____

_____

_____

_____

_____

_____

_____

_____

_____

_____

1 Tell a partner an interesting fact about an animal. What is your favorite animal?

2 Write the plan below as a paragraph.

Plan	Paragraph
Main idea: Largest land mammals on earth.	Elephants are the largest land mammals on earth.
Detail: Long trunks to pick up food.	
Detail: Large ears help them to keep cool.	
Final sentence: Some are as tall as 3 metres.	

3 Add interesting details to the plan below, using **nouns** and **adjectives**. Then write it out as a paragraph.

| teeth | fast | fin | sharp |

Plan	Paragraph
Main idea: Sharks are very good hunters.	
Detail:	
Detail:	
Final sentence: Sharks rarely attack humans.	

4 Choose a different animal. Plan and write a paragraph about it, using nouns and adjectives.

| tall | long | small | fast | slow | neck | paws | wings | tail |

Plan	Paragraph
Main idea:	
Detail:	
Detail:	
Final sentence:	

1 Draw a new animal. Then give your animal a name.

Name: _____

2 Match the **nouns** to their meanings.

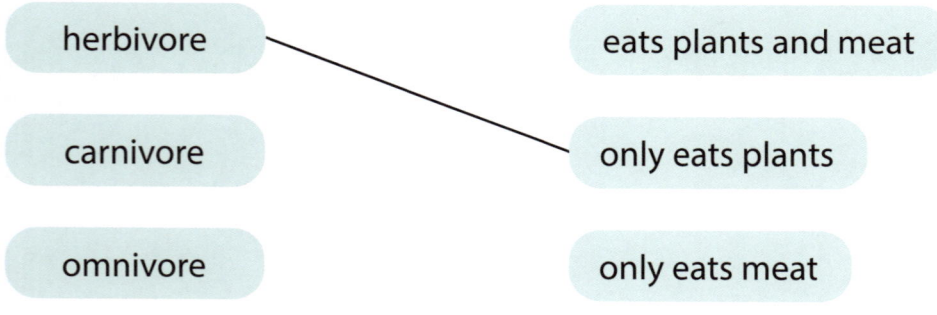

herbivore   eats plants and meat

carnivore   only eats plants

omnivore   only eats meat

Complete the sentence using one of the nouns.

My new animal is _____

Complete the sentence to say what your new animal's favourite food is.

Its favourite food is _____

_____

3 Match the habitats to their meanings.

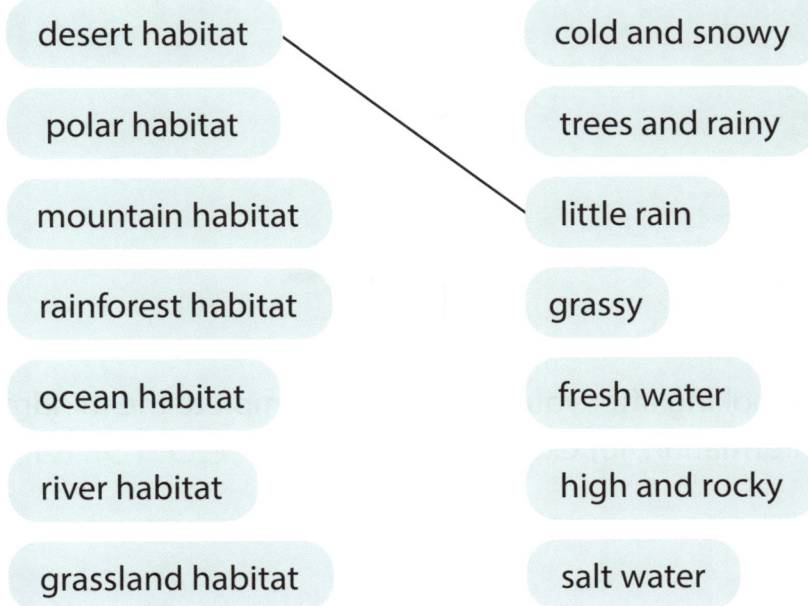

desert habitat   cold and snowy

polar habitat   trees and rainy

mountain habitat   little rain

rainforest habitat   grassy

ocean habitat   fresh water

river habitat   high and rocky

grassland habitat   salt water

4 Write a paragraph describing your new animal in detail. Use the words 'herbivore', 'carnivore' or 'omnivore' and give information about its habitat.

1 If you could have any animal as a pet, what would you choose?
Discuss how you would look after your chosen pet.

2 You are going to write a report on looking after your chosen pet. Complete the mindmap with the title, subheadings and information, for example, Food: Feed tortoise every day.

Here are some possible subheadings:

| Behaviour | Food | Exercise | Likes and dislikes | Keeping clean |

Title:

3 Why do writers use subheadings?

_____

_____

4 Write a report about looking after your pet. Use your title and subheadings to organize the information.

Title: Looking after cats

Subheading: Likes and dislikes

Although cats drink water, they dislike getting wet.

_____

_____

_____

_____

_____

_____

_____

_____

1 Discuss the new product in the picture.
Would you use it? What would you call it?

helmet

rocket boost

floating ball

2 Match the product features below to the product.

Product features	**Product**

This product will help to:
- stop tooth decay
- make your breath fresh.

football

Description
- It's round and bouncy.
- You can use it to play many different games.

sunscreen

When to use
- Use this product when the sun is strong.
- You must reapply it every few hours.

toothpaste

3 Plan a report on the new product in **1**. Use subheadings and add ideas using bullet points.

Product name: _____

Description

- _____

- _____

How to be safe

- _____
- _____

When to use

- _____
- _____

How this product will help you

- _____
- _____

4 Write your report.

| fast | float | hover | soar | steer | work | traffic jam | park | travel |

Title: _____

Subheading: _____

_____

_____

_____

_____

_____

1 This is Kabir. He has just won a medal. What do you think he won it for?
There is a clue below...

2 Complete the table using the information below and your own ideas.

on 26 June   on the school playing field   ~~Kabir~~   won a medal

Who?	Kabir
What?	
When?	
Where?	

3 Circle the **adverbs of time** in the newspaper report.

(Yesterday,) Kabir was just another athlete. Few people had heard his name. All that changed today. He was awarded a gold medal for long jump. Kabir practises daily. He hopes to win more medals soon.

Jumping for gold!
Kabir grabs the top prize!
Gold for Kabir

Circle the newspaper heading you like best.

4 Write a newspaper article to describe Kabir's win. Write the events in order. Include adverbs of time and as much detail as possible.

| on 26 June | at 11am | two hours later | after school | finally | next |
| soon | after that | eventually | immediately | straight away | |

At 11am on 26 June, Kabir was waiting to take the biggest jump of his life. First, he warmed up.

1 Ask a partner questions about what they'd like to be when they're older.

2 Match each sentence to the correct punctuation mark.

I want to be a famous scientist

Footballers are the best

Why do you want to be famous

Have you always wanted to write books

I'm going to be the fastest runner ever

I'd like to be a doctor or an artist

I want to travel the world

?

.

!

3 Write three questions and answers from **1**. Can you include an exclamation in one of the answers?

Questions	Answers
What do you want to be when you grow up?	One day, I want to be a teacher.

Questions	Answers

4 Write a report on what you want to be when you're older and why. Remember to punctuate it correctly.

4 Games, poems and plays

1 Say and write the plural name for each of the foods below.

	Singular	Plural
	orange	
	ice cream	
	cherry	
	raspberry	

2 Change these **nouns** to plurals. Add them to the correct place in the table.

dog   family   wife   shelf   flash   box   city

leaf   baby   apple   pen   bus

Add -s	Add -es	Drop the -y Add -ies	Drop the -f or -fe Add -ves
dogs	flashes	babies	shelves

3 Match the nouns to their plurals. Then add to them to the list poem.

goose	teeth	Ten terrific
foot	geese	Nine gorgeous
child	mice	Eight mini
fish	children	Seven cheerful
tooth	sheep	Six silly
scarf	wolves	Five wild
woman	feet	Four fast
sheep	women	Three whispering
wolf	scarves	Two silk
mouse	fish	One friendly

teeth _____

_____

_____

_____

_____

_____

_____

_____

_____

_____

4 Write your own list poem about things you might find at school.

Ten purple pencils _____

Nine _____

Eight _____

Seven _____

Six _____

Five _____

Four _____

Three _____

Two _____

One _____

1 Discuss what these gibbons like to do.

2 Change these **verbs** so they end in -ing. Add them to the correct place in the table.

~~sit~~	jump	skip	grab	~~play~~	race	swing
slip	~~chase~~	smile	climb	bite		

Add -ing	Drop the -e Add -ing	Double the last letter Add -ing
playing	chasing	sitting

3 This poem has five lines with different numbers of words in each line.
It uses adjectives and verbs to describe an animal.

Cat
Cute, furry
Licking, eating, playing
Asleep on my pillow
Purr

> **1** word for name of animal

> **2** adjectives

> **3** -ing verbs

> **4**-word description

> **1** word

Add two -ing verbs to this poem about a gibbon.

Gibbon

Noisy, playful

Jumping, _____ , _____

High in the trees

Happy

4 Write your own poem about any animal.

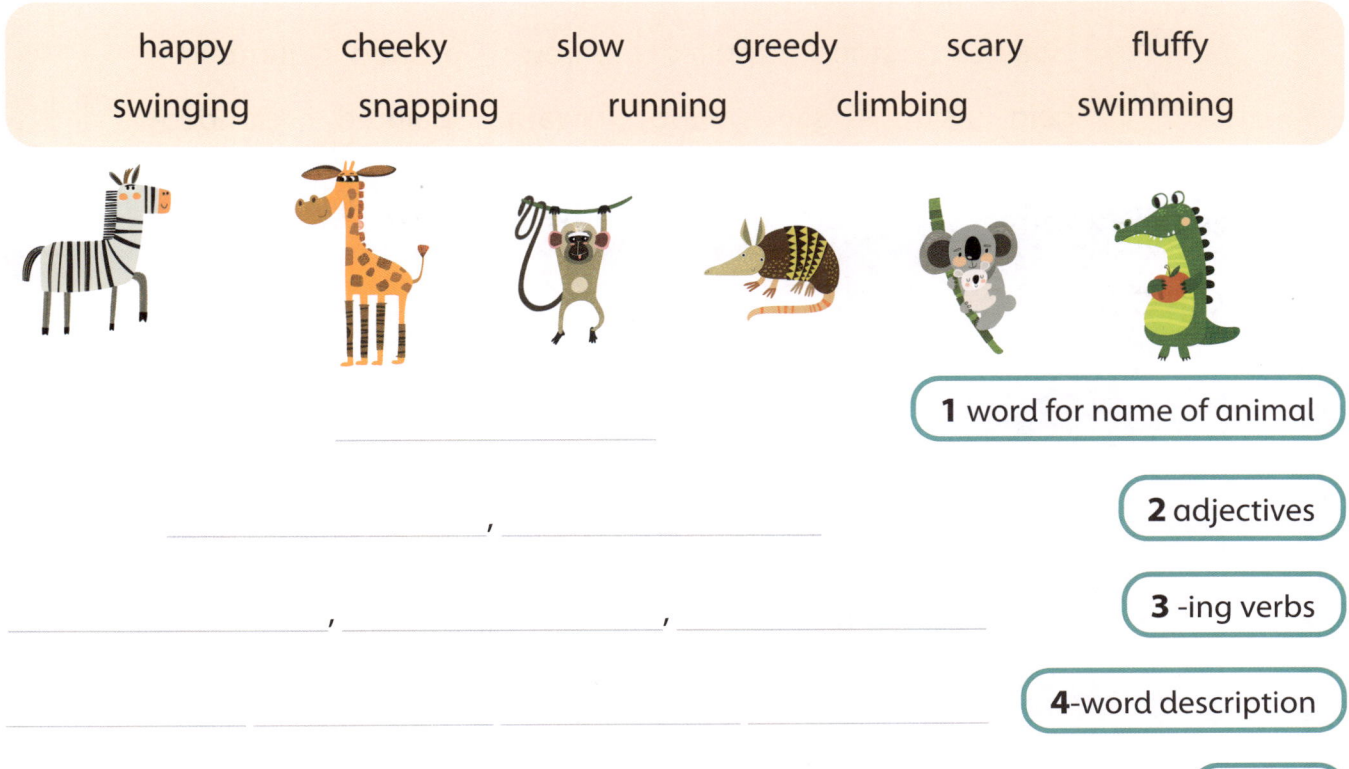

| happy | cheeky | slow | greedy | scary | fluffy |
| swinging | snapping | running | climbing | swimming |

_____

_____ , _____

_____ , _____ , _____

> **1** word for name of animal

> **2** adjectives

> **3** -ing verbs

> **4**-word description

> **1** word

1 Act out one of the **verbs** below for a partner. Can your partner guess which one it is?

Open

Fall

Show

Pay

Create

Catch

2 Complete the table using these verbs.

~~walked~~   stood   pulled   threw   pushed   jumped

held   slept   sat   ~~hung~~   swam   painted   climbed

regular -ed verbs	irregular verbs
walked	hung

3 Match each irregular verb to its **past tense**.

run   saw

fall   ran

fly   froze

see   flew

fight   fought

freeze   fell

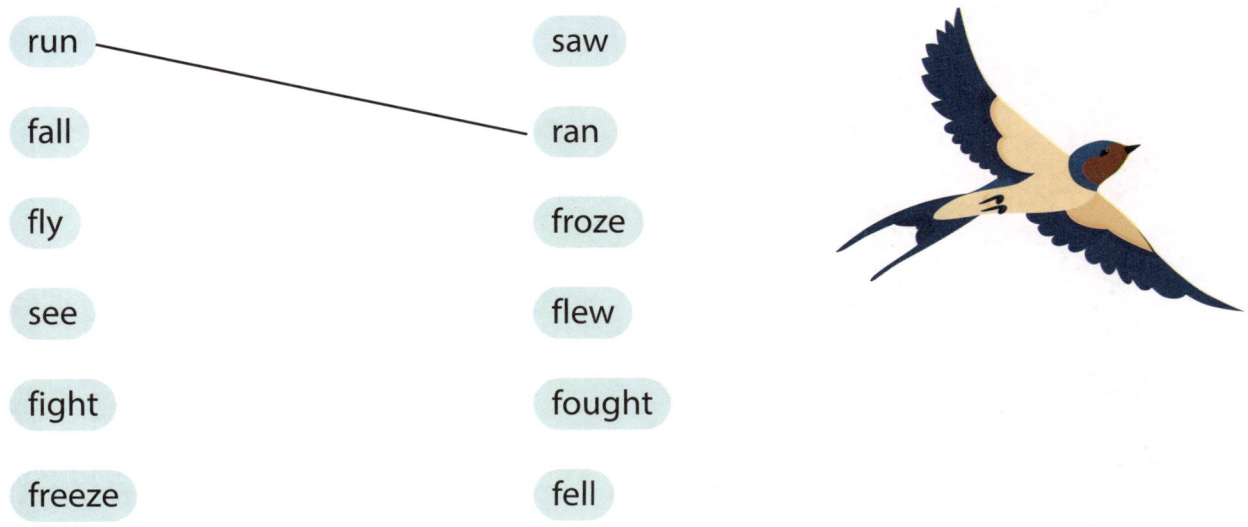

4 Play 'Two facts and a fiction'. Write down three memories. Two should be true and one should be made up. Read them to a partner. Can they spot the fiction?

1 _____

2 _____

3 _____

Write down one memory in more detail.

_____

_____

_____

_____

_____

_____

_____

Underline the regular verbs and circle the irregular verbs. How many verbs did you use? _____

1 You have 5 minutes to play 'Spot the difference'.
Circle any differences you see. There are six to find!

2 Write sentences about some of the differences you found. Use **prepositions**.

on	beside	under	above

There is a dragonfly **on** the leaf.

3 Rewrite each sentence with the prepositional phrase at the start.
Don't forget the comma!

A mouse hid under a tree. Under a tree, a mouse hid.

a It was warm beside the fire.

_____

b Some clouds floated in the sky.

_____

c The cat slept on the sofa.

_____

d Birds flew above the trees.

_____

4 This picture is going to be made into a 'Spot the difference' game. Describe five changes that could be made to the picture. Use prepositions.

On the chair, add a book.

_____

_____

_____

_____

_____

1 Read the story of *The Ant and the Dove*. Discuss what happens.

One day, Dove noticed an ant drowning in the water. She dropped a leaf into the water. Ant climbed onto the leaf and was saved!

"Thank you!" cried Ant. "You saved me!"

"You're welcome," said Dove with a smile.

Just then, Ant noticed a hunter. The hunter was creeping up to Dove and was about to catch her in his net. Quick as a flash, Ant bit the hunter on his toe.

"Ouch!" yelled the hunter, dropping his net.

Dove flew off. Ant smiled. He was pleased that he could help Dove in return for her kindness.

2 Complete the playscript using these **adverbs**.

> gratefully   ~~fearfully~~   happily   quickly

Ant: (*fearfully*) Help me! I'm drowning!

Dove: (*picks a leaf and* _____ *flies over to ant*) Climb onto this!

Ant: (_____) Thank you, Dove. You saved my life!

Dove: (_____ *flies up to a branch*) You're welcome!

3 Finish the playscript. Can you include an adverb?

_____

_____

_____

_____

4 Write your own playscript. Try to include some adverbs.

> sadly   hungrily   excitedly   carefully   gently   angrily

_____

_____

_____

_____

_____

_____

1 Discuss this picture. What might the children be saying or thinking?

2 Choose a name, speech verb and speech. Write lines of speech below, punctuating them correctly.

Name	Speech verb	Speech
Zahid	asked,	"I think it's almost the end of break."
Luis	stated,	"I wish I had someone to play with."
Mali	mumbled,	"Will you pass me the ball?"
Pablo	shouted,	"I'm right behind you!"

Mali stated, "I think it's almost the end of break."

3 Add the missing punctuation to the speech below.

Hamad shouted "Look, I've rolled a six!

Gabriel asked Is it my turn next?"

I never win," moaned Lu

Hamad said, You should be blue next time.

4 Choose characters from the picture above, or make up your own characters. Write a conversation between them.

shrieked	whispered	explained	cried	argued	muttered

"Do you want to play with us?" asked Afrin.

_____

_____

_____

_____

_____

_____

_____

_____

_____

_____

1 Discuss this picture.
What do you think happened?

2 We call these **co-ordinating conjunctions** 'FANBOYS' to help us remember them. Look at them for 1 minute. Then cover them up and write as many as you can remember.

for	and	nor	but	or	yet	so
F	**A**	**N**	**B**	**O**	**Y**	**S**

F _____

A _____

N _____

B _____

O _____

Y _____

S _____

3 Join the sentences together using a co-ordinating conjunction. Don't forget the comma!

The cat was stuck in the tree. Arjun had to climb up.

The cat was stuck in the tree, **so** Arjun had to climb up.

a Arjun might save the cat. It might climb down itself.

_____

_____

b The cat liked climbing. It didn't like being stuck.

_____

_____

Finish each sentence.

c The cat got stuck in the tree, and _____

d Arjun used a ladder, but _____

e It was lucky Mia was there, for _____

4 Write sentences about this picture. Use a co-ordinating conjunction in each sentence. Can you use them all?

_____

_____

_____

_____

_____

_____

_____

_____

Vocabulary

pawprints

mess

chaos

splat

spilled

wall

1 Talk about what is happening in the picture.
How does Leo feel? Who might his mum be calling?

2 We call these **subordinating conjunctions** 'BABIES' to help us remember them. Look at them for 1 minute. Then cover them up and write as many as you can remember.

| B | because | A | as | B | before | I | if | E | even though | S | since |

B _____   **I** _____

A _____   **E** _____

B _____   **S** _____

3 Choose the best subordinating conjunction to fill each gap.

The dolphin was swimming ___*before*___ it got stuck on the sand. (before/because)

a They might save the dolphin _____ Mum calls for help. (if/as)

b _____ it was cold, Leo was glad he had a coat. (since/even though)

Finish these sentences, then circle the subordinating conjunctions.

Leo frowned (because) he was worried about the dolphin.

d   The dolphin was alive, even though _____

e   As they loved dolphins, Leo and his mum _____

f   If the dolphin didn't get back in the water, _____

4   Look at this picture and write what happened next.
Use 'BABIES' subordinating conjunctions.

_____

_____

_____

_____

_____

_____

_____

_____

_____

_____

💬 **1** Do you have a friend or family member you don't see very often? Talk to a partner about them.

2 Add the correct punctuation to this letter.

1 Old Street

Old Town

Dear Zara,

How are you **?**

I miss you at school____ I haven't seen you for a whole year____

I am writing to tell you our news____ We went on holiday and it was so fun____ Miriam and I spent every day in the pool____ We had yummy food in a café and we played games with the other children____

I am reading a good book called 'The Boy and his Horse'____

What are you doing____ Do you like your new school____

Write back soon____

Kimi

3 You are going to write a letter to your friend or family member. What do you want to tell them? Do you have any questions to ask them?

4 Write your letter. Include the school address at the top.

1 Imagine that you are at this party!
Discuss these questions:

- What would you eat?
- What games would you play?
- What music would you dance to?

2 Which **contraction** could you use instead of the underlined words?
Draw a line to match them up.

<u>They are</u> having a party.	He's
<u>She is</u> holding strawberries.	They're
<u>He is</u> playing a game.	I'm
<u>We are</u> dancing.	We're
<u>I am</u> holding a balloon.	She's

3 Complete the tables. Write these contractions out in full.

Contraction	Full words
you're	you are
he's	
it's	
I've	

Contraction	Full words
isn't	
can't	
they'll	
she's	

Write a sentence about the party using one of the contractions above.

_____

_____

4 Imagine that you have gone to a fancy dress party. Describe what you're wearing and who you dressed up as. Describe the party. Use at least three contractions.

_____

_____

_____

_____

_____

_____

_____

1 Discuss this picture. What might Tam be thinking? What might Tam's aunt be thinking? Would you eat one of these cupcakes?

Tam

Tam's aunt

2 Circle the **verb** in each sentence. Tick to say whether it is in the **past tense** or the **present tense**.

	Past tense	Present tense
Tam (baked) cupcakes.	✓	
Tam's aunt tries a cupcake.		
Tam enjoyed baking.		
Tam's mum sees the messy kitchen.		
Tam helped his mum to wash up.		

3   Use these past tense verbs to write some sentences about Tam and his aunt.

wore	cleaned	tried	giggled	ate

Tam wore a red and grey top.

_____

_____

_____

_____

4   When was the last time something made you laugh a lot?
Describe it in detail using the past tense.

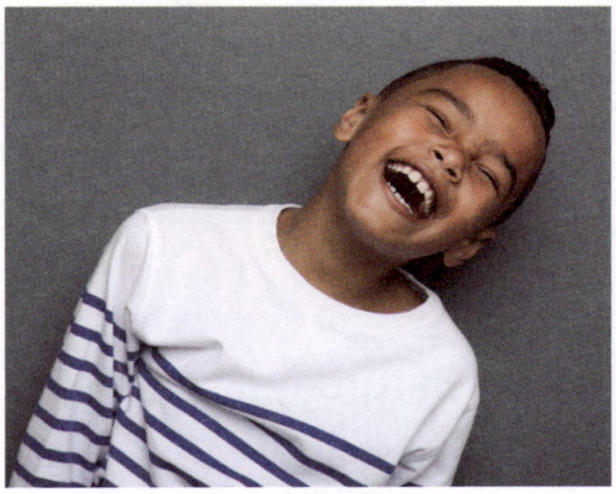

The last time something made me

laugh a lot was when _____

_____

_____

_____

_____

_____

_____

_____

1 Discuss what you have done over the last week. It could be activities in school or at home. It could be a book or game you have enjoyed.

2 Match these diary entries to the correct headings.

Heading	Diary entry
Saturday	We went on a school trip on Thursday.
Sunday	The school week began with an assembly.
Monday	My weekend started with a drama class.
Tuesday	On Sunday afternoon, we visited my grandma.
Wednesday	At the end of the school week, we had fish for lunch.
Thursday	In the middle of the school week, we had a sports lesson.
Friday	We went to my uncle's house for tea on Tuesday.

3 Make notes about what you have done over the last week.

-

4 Write a diary entry for two days from the last week. Include lots of detail about what you did and how you felt about it.

6 Writing to persuade

1 Imagine that you are in this picture. Discuss what you would see, feel and hear.

2 Replace the underlined **nouns** and **adjectives** with words from the box.

icy	glow	sandy shore	delicious	~~soft~~

Listen to the <u>gentle</u> sound of the waves.

Listen to the **soft** sound of the waves.

a Eat a <u>tasty</u> ice cream.

_____

b Walk on the <u>beach</u>.

_____

c Dip your feet in the <u>cold</u> water.

_____

d Feel the warm <u>light</u> of the sun.

_____

3 Finish these sentences using nouns and adjectives.

~~amazing~~   ~~sandcastle~~   noisy   seagulls   rippling   ocean

swaying   palm trees   turquoise   water

We built an amazing sandcastle.

I swam _____

_____

I looked up and saw _____

_____

4 Write a postcard telling your friend about your holiday. Use adjectives.

POSTCARD

Dear _____

_____

_____

_____

_____

_____

_____

From _____

1 Which of these do you prefer?

sun	☀	or	rain	🌧
ice cream	🍦	or	pizza	🍕
football	⚽	or	cricket	🏏
the forest	🌲	or	the park	🏞

2 Write sentences explaining your choices. Use 'prefer' and 'because'.

I **prefer** rain **because** I like to jump in puddles.

3 Rewrite the sentences with the **subordinate clause** at the beginning.

I love cricket, <u>even though I was hit by the ball</u>.

Even though I was hit by the ball, I love cricket.

a I like the rain, <u>despite the grey clouds</u>.

_____

_____

b Football is fun, <u>even though I'm not very good at it</u>.

_____

_____

4 Would you prefer to fly or turn invisible? Write a paragraph to convince your teacher. Use the **subordinating conjunctions** 'because', 'although', 'if'.

| zoom | soar | clouds | birds | listen | spy | sneak | creep |

_____

_____

_____

_____

_____

1 Discuss these pictures. What is behind the door?
Is it safe to go in? How might you use the key?

2 With a partner, discuss reasons to go through the door and reasons not to.
Complete the table.

exciting	scary	spooky	key	mysterious

Reasons to go in	Reasons not to go in
The sign says 'welcome'.	We don't know who lives there.

3 Decide whether you should or shouldn't go through the door. Circle 'should' or 'shouldn't' in the first sentence. Then explain your decision using the **adverbs**.

I think we should / shouldn't go in.

Firstly,

Also,

Finally,

4 You find a mysterious box in the forest. Decide whether to take it or leave it. Explain your reasons using the adverbs 'Firstly', 'Also' and 'Finally'.

1 Which animal would make the best pet and why?

| cutest | scarier | easiest | slowest | sweetest | fluffier |

2 **Exaggeration** makes something seem bigger, better or worse than it really is. Complete each **simile** by choosing the most exaggerated ending.

My horse is as fast as _a motorbike._

| a motorbike | a skateboard | a pushbike |

a My cat is as soft as _____

| a cloud | the fluffiest cloud | a fluffy cloud |

b My dog is as slow as _____

| the laziest snail | a snail | a lazy snail |

c My bird's song is as sweet as _____

| music | the best music in the world | nice music |

3 Finish the sentences with exaggeration.

My fish is so clever, he could do my maths homework for me.

a My rabbit is so fast, he could _____

_____

b My hamster is so strong, she could _____

_____

c My bird is so greedy, she could _____

_____

4 This is Superfrog. She can run! She can swim! She can dance!
She can fly! Describe Superfrog using similes and exaggeration.

as fast as	speediest	so good at dancing
zooms up like	flies faster than	swims like

_____

_____

_____

_____

_____

_____

1 These children want to persuade their teacher to give them longer break times. Discuss what they might be saying. Then write it in the speech bubbles.

2 The mistakes in these sentences are circled. Write the corrections in the boxes above.

| | | . |

"ⓘ think we should play more sports at school❓" said Yasmeena.

| |

a "Your lessons are more important,◯ stated the teacher.

| | |

b ◯Yes, although exercise is good for us!◯ replied Carmel.

| | |

c "ⓘt is very good for you◯" agreed the teacher.

3 Rewrite the sentences below with speech marks and a different speech **verb** to replace 'said'.

> asked   ~~sighed~~   shouted   stated

I wish we had longer breaks, said Yasmeena.

"I wish we had longer breaks," sighed Yasmeena.

a Why can't we have longer to play? said Carmel.

_____

b We should have longer breaks from learning, said Rashid.

_____

c I love break time! said Lena.

_____

4 Luis wants to eat at a restaurant, but Arjun wants to go to the cinema. Write their conversation. Use more interesting words than 'said'.

"Don't you feel hungry?" asked Luis.

_____

_____

_____

_____

_____

1 Talk about a book you have enjoyed.
Write its title and add a drawing.

2 Who is the main character? _____

Write a sentence using **adjectives** to describe the main character.

| adventurous | honest | naughty | funny | brave | kind |

The main character is _____

_____

Describe what the story is about.

_____

_____

_____

3 What do you like about the book?

_____

Is there anything you don't like about the book? _____

_____

_____

4 Who else do you think would enjoy this book?

I think _____

_____

_____

What would you rate this book?

I would rate this book _____ out of 10 because _____

_____

_____

Describe your favourite part of the book.

_____

_____

_____

_____

_____

_____

adjective a describing word like **big, exciting** or **unexpected**. They describe nouns (people, places, animals, things).

- The dragon's claws were **curved** and **sharp**.
- It had **scaly** skin and **massive** eyes.

adverb of manner adds information to verbs. It tells us *how* the action happens.

- She sang **loudly**.
- **Carefully** wash the glasses.
- He **quickly** hid the book.

adverb of place adds information to verbs. It tells us *where* the action happens.

- **Outside**, it was raining.
- The dog slept **downstairs**.

adverb of time adds information to verbs. It tells us *when* the action happens.

- We are leaving **soon**.
- **First**, read the instructions.

co-ordinating conjunction a word that links two parts of a sentence which make sense on their own. The co-ordinating conjunctions are: **for, and, nor, but, or, yet, so**.

- It was cold, **but** I had a warm coat.
- We can stay here, **or** we can go to the park.
- It had been a long journey, **so** I was tired.

contraction two words shortened to one. It has an apostrophe to replace missing letters.

- I **didn't** go because **it's** boring.

did not   it is

direct speech the actual words a person says. There are speech marks at the beginning and end of direct speech.

- "Can I talk to you please?" asked Hana.

exaggeration this makes something sound better or worse than it is.

- It was **hotter than the sun** outside.
- This homework will take **forever**.

metaphor a way of describing something by saying it is something else.

- The **sun** is a **yellow beach ball**.
- Thanks for your help. **You are a star!**

noun the name of a person, place, animal or thing. Nouns can be singular (when there is just one) or plural (when there are more than one).

- **Luc** saw a **fox** and a **chicken** at the **farm**.
- The **boys** saw four **foxes** and two **chickens** at the **farm**.

past tense tells us that something has already happened.

- I **played** a game yesterday.
- I **slipped** in the mud earlier today.

possessive pronoun shows ownership of something and is a way of avoiding repeating someone's name; the possessive pronouns are: **mine, her, his, theirs, ours, its, yours**.

preposition a linking word that describes where something is in time or space.

- The coat is **on** the chair.
- Dad is **behind** the tree.

present tense tells us that something is happening now.

- I **am playing** a game now.

- She **runs** across the playground.

pronoun a word that takes the place of a noun or proper noun **(me, herself, his, yours)**.

- A teacher saw Dara using a phone. As **she** was a student, **he** took **it** away.

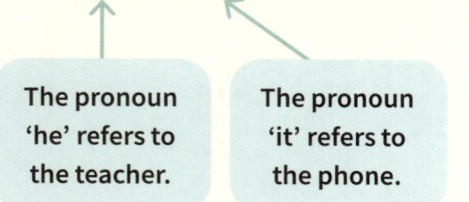

The pronoun 'he' refers to the teacher.

The pronoun 'it' refers to the phone.

The pronoun 'she' refers to Dara.

simile a way of describing something by comparing it to something else. Similes use the words 'as' or 'like'.

- **He was as brave as a lion** at the dentist.

- The **sun is like a yellow beach ball**.

subordinate clause a group of words that adds information to the main clause. It can't be used as a sentence on its own. It begins with a subordinate conjunction.

- **When I finish my homework,** I will go and meet my friends.

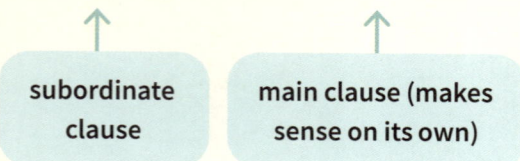

subordinate clause

main clause (makes sense on its own)

subordinating conjunction a word that introduces a subordinate (less important) clause. Some examples are: **if, as, because, when, until**.

- You can go out **if** you finish your dinner.
- **As** you are tired, you should go to bed.
- We stopped playing football **because** it was getting dark.

synonym a word that has the same meaning as another word.

- **Shut** the door!

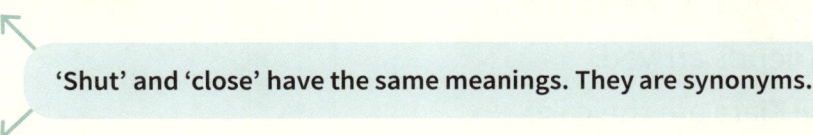

'Shut' and 'close' have the same meanings. They are synonyms.

- **Close** the door!

verb a doing word **(play, jump)** or a being word **(am, is, are, was, were)**. Past tense verbs can be regular (end in -ed) or irregular (don't end in -ed).

- They **eat** slowly.

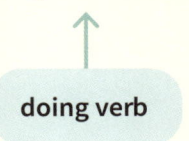

doing verb

- I **am** hungry.

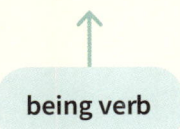

being verb

- The boys **ran** down the hill as it **rained**.

irregular verb   regular verb

1 Underline the main clause in each sentence below.

The house was quiet because the children were at school.

The sun came out when we were at the park.

While it slept, the cat snored.

Before I went to bed, I brushed my teeth.

The sailors waited as the storm moved closer.

2 Underline the subordinate clause in each sentence below.

The classroom was noisy until the teacher arrived.

If you finish your homework, you can watch a film.

The party started when his friends arrived.

Although she wasn't hungry, Kiara ate the cake.

Hassan hasn't played cricket since he hurt his knee.

3 Underline the conjunction in each sentence. Circle 'C' if it is a co-ordinating conjunction or 'S' if it is a subordinating conjunction.

Tam went to the shop and bought a magazine.	C or S
I don't like cats because they make me sneeze.	C or S
Go back to class when you hear the bell.	C or S
We can go now, or we can leave later.	C or S
Zara picked some apples, but some of them were rotten.	C or S
Although it was late, I wasn't tired.	C or S

4 Circle the irregular past tense verbs.

slept   smiled   raced   sang

laughed   ate   stretched   wrote

got   bought   jogged   skipped